PHYCOLOGY
of
Money
and
Wealth

Facts and principles of getting rich and staying rich.

By

Todd L. Craft

Table of Contents

ABOUT MONEY AND WEALTH PHYCOLOGY

The theory of money is a field of financial matters that concentrates on the capabilities, beginnings, and utilization of money. Money is a mechanism of trade that is utilized to work with exchanges between financial specialists. It permits individuals to exchange labor and products without bargaining, which is the immediate trade of one great or administration for another. The theory of money is significant on the grounds that it assists us with understanding how money is made, the way things are utilized, and what it means for the economy.

Brain research is the investigation of the psyche and conduct, and it very well may be applied to a wide range of parts of life, including money and money. The mental elements that impact our relationship with money are complicated and can change significantly from one individual to another. Certain individuals might be inspired by the craving for riches and material belongings, while others might put a higher worth on encounters and individual satisfaction. There is a wide range of mental hypotheses and variables that can impact our perspectives and ways of behaving with regard to money, including our childhood, our qualities, and our own encounters.

FACTORS THAT INFLUENCES MONEY PHYCOLOGY

There is a wide range of elements that can influence the brain research of money, including our childhood, our qualities, and our own encounters. A few different elements that can impact our mentalities and ways of behaving toward money include:

Our family and social foundation: how we were raised and the qualities that were imparted to us by our folks and social childhood can significantly impact our perspectives and ways of behaving towards money.

Our own encounters: Our own encounters with money, like our most memorable work or our most memorable significant buy, can likewise shape our mentalities and ways of behaving towards it.

Our emotions: Our emotions can likewise assume a part in our mentalities and ways of behaving towards money. For instance, assuming we are feeling worried or restless, we might be bound to settle on hasty monetary choices.

Our convictions and values: Our convictions and values can likewise impact our perspectives and ways of behaving towards money. For instance, assuming that we esteem encounters over material belongings, we might be less inclined to burn money on material things and be bound to save it for movement or different encounters.

Our social and companion impacts: Our companions and groups of friends can likewise impact our mentalities and ways of behaving towards money. For instance, on the off chance that our companions are burning through money on extravagant things, we might feel strain to do likewise, regardless of whether it's not in accordance with our own qualities or monetary objectives.

DEVELOPING POSITIVITY ABOUT MONEY

Having a positive brain research of money can assist you with pursuing better monetary choices and leading an all the more monetarily sound and satisfying life. The following are a couple of ways to foster a positive brain research of money:

Teach yourself: Understanding the rudiments of individual budgets and contributing can assist you with pursuing better monetary choices and feeling more sure and in charge of your money.

Put forth clear monetary objectives: Distinguishing your monetary objectives and making an arrangement to accomplish them can assist you with keeping on track and inspired.

Practice care: Care is the act of being available and mindful at the time, without judgement. With regards to money, this implies monitoring your ways of managing money and making cognizant, intentional decisions about how you utilize your money. In other words, be responsible.

Keep away from enthusiastic spending: Impulsive spending can prompt monetary issues and sensations of disappointment. On the off chance that you end up making indiscreet buys, attempt to make a stride back and consider whether the buy is truly vital or lines up with your monetary objectives.

Look for help: In the event that you're battling with monetary pressure or negative perspectives towards money, think about looking for help from a monetary counsel, specialist, or care group. Discussing your interests and getting direction from experts can assist you to foster a better relationship with money.

money Fascination

The idea of money fascination, otherwise called the "pattern of good following good," depends on the possibility that individuals can draw in riches and overflow into their lives by zeroing in on their viewpoints and energy on abundance and overflow. This thought is frequently connected with new age development and isn't upheld by standard financial hypotheses.

Advocates of money fascination contend that individuals can show their monetary objectives by utilizing the influence of their psyches to draw in abundance. They trust that by imagining riches, zeroing in on good considerations and sentiments about money, and making a move to show their objectives, they can draw overflow into their lives.

In any case, there is no proof to help the possibility that money fascination is a legitimate method for drawing in riches. As a matter of fact, most financial specialists would contend that singular's not entirely settled by a mix of variables, including their schooling, abilities, experience, and the open doors accessible to them in the economy. Moreover, the possibility of money fascination might be destructive on the grounds that it can persuade individuals to think that they don't have to try sincerely or foster the vital abilities to accomplish their monetary objectives. All things considered, they might be persuaded to think that they can essentially think their direction to riches, which isn't sensible.

In conclusion, the possibility of money fascination isn't upheld by standard monetary theory and is certainly not a substantial method for drawing in riches. All things considered, making monetary progress requires difficult work, devotion, and a sound comprehension of financial matters and individual budgets.

BECOMING WEALTHY

Independent affluent individuals don't become rich coincidentally. All things considered, they frequently make purposeful moves to bring in money and create financial momentum. In the event that you're prepared to assume command over your funds, picking and focusing on a bit-by-bit plan frequently helps increment your riches.

Recognize your objectives:
Before you begin becoming rich, devise a monetary arrangement. The following are a couple of inquiries you might pose to yourself as you set up your arrangement:
What does being rich mean? Are there specific total assets I might want to hit?
What is my month-to-month financial plan objective? Am I hoping to set money aside to contribute or to take care of obligations?
Am I hoping to accomplish exiting the workforce?

Get explicit with your responses so you know your accurate objectives. When you have your 10,000-foot view vision laid out, separate it into more modest transient objectives that are simpler to accomplish. By making this guide, you ought to have a more clear feeling of what your objective is and how to arrive.

End debts of high interest rates:
Nothing hauls down your persistent effort like an exorbitant interest obligation. Absolute buyer obligation adjustments expanded by 5.4% somewhere in the range of 2020 and 2021, as per Experian, one of the three public credit authorities. Obligations with exorbitant loan fees, for example, Visa obligations,

can be tried to take care of. In addition to the fact that you are paying the chief sum you acquired, you're many times paying powerful interest charges also.

To assume command over your obligation, begin by posting every one of your advances from the most elevated financing cost to the least. Consider making additional instalments toward the first advance sum on your exorbitant interest obligations first to limit the aggregate sum of interest you could owe when the obligation is paid off. You'll probably have to determine that the additional instalment is for the first credit sum — inquire as to whether there is a sure cycle you ought to follow while utilizing this methodology.

Whenever you've taken care of that first obligation in full, continue on toward the credit with the second most elevated financing cost. You're spending less money on revenue charges and keeping more money in your pocket by focusing on high-rate obligations.

Begin planning and setting aside money:

To take care of obligations and hit your monetary objectives, it's vital to figure out how to deal with your money. Follow these moves toward carrying out an essential planning plan:

Distinguish costs: Record your revenue sources and costs and work out the amount you make or spend on normal for everything on your rundown.

Monitor significant spending classifications: Inspect the amount you spend every month on classifications like lease, utilities, and food. Remember to likewise represent optional spending, for example, eating out or purchasing another book.

Search for regions to get to the next level: When you have a higher perspective of your month-to-month income, find spots where you can scale back to set aside additional money.

Perhaps you can cook at home more frequently than eating out at cafés. Or on the other hand, maybe there are free exercises you can do in your space to save on diversion. Utilize the reserve funds you make to fabricate a backup stash, grow savings, pay down obligations, or even contribute.

Pay yourself first:

Without enough money for crises, you risk getting into an intense monetary spot on the off chance that an unforeseen cost emerges. In the event that you don't have money close by, you might charge the cost to your Mastercard or apply for a new line of credit, further affecting your funds by expanding your obligation.

To reinforce your reserve funds, try to pay yourself first. This implies saving a piece of your regularly scheduled check to place into an investment account, so you don't spend it somewhere else.

You might try and robotize this cycle so that it's finished before the money opens up to spend. You could set up a programmed move from your financial records to a bank account. In the event that your boss proposes a direct store for your check, you might decide to part the store, with a piece of your check going straightforwardly into a bank account and the rest of your financial records.

Start investing:

Investing money is in many cases one of the most mind-blowing ways of creating financial stability. After some time, it is fruitful to accept your speculations. In the event that you keep all of your money in a fundamental ledger, you risk degrading your money because of expansion. Speculations are much of the time a more intelligent method for saving.

Put resources into stocks, common assets or trade exchanged reserves (ETFs) to join the market as soon as could be expected and exploit the force of compound returns.

For instance, suppose you contribute $1,000 each month beginning at age 30. With a 7% pace of return, you'd have more than $170,000 following 10 years, $500,000 following 20 years, and $1.15 million following 30 years. The previous you contribute, the additional time you need to procure and accumulate interest.

There are two primary record classes for putting money in the financial exchange:

You can utilize charge-advantaged retirement accounts, for example, a business-supported 401(k) or an IRA.

You can utilize one of the most amazing investment funds like Reserve, Advancement, or SoFi.

Unbelievable financial backer Warren Buffett suggests starting with a broadened portfolio by including ETFs that track significant securities exchange files, like the S&P; 500.

If you add to a 401(k) plan, exploit any business match benefits on a piece of your commitments. The matched sum addresses a prompt 100 percent profit from your speculation, so it merits maximizing it whenever the situation allows.

You can likewise carefully select stocks, securities, and other speculation vehicles, albeit this might expand your gamble and affect your venture system.

Tip:

Contributing consistently involves some gambling, however assuming that you contribute as long as possible, you might have the option to climate the promising and less promising times of the market yet dominate the competition.

Multiply your income:

There's just such a lot of money you can save with the pay you have. To speed up your obligation result and increment your venture commitments, search for ways of bringing in money and increment what you procure. For instance:

If you are happy with your ongoing manager: Think about requesting a raise or pursuing an advancement.

Talk with your director about your professional objectives and figure out what steps you can take to advance toward them.

On the off chance that you are available to search for another position: Think about taking a course or procuring a confirmation that could place you in the running for a situation with a higher check. Make a point to haggle any proposition for employment before tolerating it.

Besides your essential pay, you can likewise think about perhaps the best side gig. Whether you drive for Uber, are independent on the web, or begin a blog, there are numerous imaginative ways of transforming your ability and innovative soul into additional pay.

Have the right attitude:

Assuming you're utilized to monetary battle, you probably won't accept that becoming affluent is workable for you. This restricting conviction makes each step considerably harder to accomplish.

That is the reason developing a substantial financial foundation outlook is crucial for figuring out how to become rich. It might take reliable, deliberate work to find success and develop your abundance.

It is not necessarily the case that there aren't imbalances in the public eye or that everybody starts at a similar beginning line. Certain individuals face far greater fundamental deterrents than others, and a few gatherings have generally been denied chances to create financial momentum and pass it down to their relatives.

Yet, assuming you accept that becoming rich is outside the realm of possibilities for you, you may not make the strides expected to accomplish this objective. Developing an overflow attitude and relinquishing restricting convictions helps you in your endeavors to create financial momentum.

STAYING WEALTHY

In a universe of normal individuals - - and normal pay rates - - a significant number of us try to join the 7-figure club. Who doesn't fantasize about becoming affluent, so they can quit working, go on irreproachable shopping binges and take vast excursions?

Notwithstanding, most rich individuals don't do those things, and that is important for how they create and keep up with their financial well-being. There's a contrast between carrying on with an existence of thoughtless spending (which will rapidly deplete even a wealthy individual's ledger) and living for long-haul monetary freedom and riches.

The independent rich aren't more astute than any other person, however, they have dominated a few significant rules that help them excel and remain ahead. Generally significant, they treat creating financial stability as a learnable expertise and it's one that you can learn, as well.

Thus, assuming that you might want to join the positions of the very affluent, take a stab at sharpening these 10 propensities and way of life changes and see what independence from the rat race feels like.

Have a monetary development mindset:

wealthy individuals are unimaginably imaginative about pondering business and tracking down various approaches to bringing in money. Super fruitful individuals put themselves aside since they support a monetary development mentality, which changes how you view money and assists you with zeroing in on seeing beneficial open doors.

This outlook assists effective and rich individuals with accepting that there are dependably far superior ventures to chip away at and there's in every case more money to be made. They're available to investigate novel thoughts. They accept they're consistently equipped for making changes and making positive results.

Network with other fruitful individuals:
Rich individuals comprehend the significance of encircling themselves with other effective individuals. Affluent individuals invest energy in organizing with other people who are rich yet additionally have a drive, ability, and, generally significant, the possibility to end up finding success. The rich invest energy consistently getting to know other similar individuals at meetings, occasions, and get-togethers, or simply snatching espresso or a beverage with somebody fascinating.

This is time admirably contributed, as it keeps their psyches zeroed in on progress and assists them with meeting new individuals who have new and provocative thoughts. Doing this likewise assists wealthy individuals to fill their contact records with applicable and compelling individuals who might help them (as well as the other way around).

Get outside your usual range of familiarity:
Rich individuals are fruitful because they have discovered that achievement arrives at the people who embrace a little uneasiness. Rich people always know that the best way to truly upgrade yourself is

to propel yourself past your cutoff points. If you have any desire to become well off, you will have to fuel your imaginative flash, think of exceptional business thoughts, and afterward go all in.

Riches and achievement don't rise out of the well-being of everyday work. They come from drawing on your internal strength and going for your huge dream. All effective business pioneers, visionaries, and huge advantages have gone past their usual ranges of familiarity to make definitive progress. Individuals who will stand out forever dared to confront their apprehensions and venture out into the unexplored world

Make numerous pay streams:
The more money you have, the simpler it is to get more money flow. Also, the most straightforward and quickest method for getting more money is to have different revenue sources. That way you generally have money coming in and can utilize the abundance of pay to put resources into new pay streams. This is the essential way the wealthy stay affluent.

There are two fundamental types of pay: dynamic pay, in which you work for the money you make, and automated revenue, in which installment isn't straightforwardly attached to the number of hours you work. Automated revenue incorporates investment property, profit stocks, list reserves, composing a book, or making an application, all of which will get a consistent progression of pay from deals or eminences.

Invest:

Rich individuals bring in their money to work for them. They realize that investing is the way to develop their funds. While keeping money for later is significant, your speculations will do the hard work to assist you with becoming affluent.

Setting aside implies placing money into a protected spot until you need to recover it, however, most investment accounts don't yield exorbitant premiums, so this heap of money fundamentally remains static - - it won't develop much past what you add. Yet, brilliant speculations will give you solid returns, which you can then reinvest. At the point when you put resources into something, you likewise acknowledge some measure of hazard, so you never need to contribute beyond what you can bear to lose.

Take calculated risks:
The wealthy don't bet on large monetary choices; they give their best to alleviate risk. They do all necessary investigation and examination and figure out which choices best suit their monetary necessities and business want. They gauge the upsides and

downsides and afterward go ahead with carefully weighed-out courses of action.

They settle on monetary choices by asking themselves, "Will this carry me nearer to my objective?" They keep away from paltry dangers that aren't exactly going to help them, and never take an unceremonious demeanour concerning money.

Centre around personal development:

Rich individuals are normally ardent perusers, however, you won't track down numerous thoughtless ocean-side books in their cabinets. The affluent grasp the significance of self-training and driving themselves to turn out to be better in all ways.

As a matter of fact, on the off chance that you take a gander at the books heaped by their beds, you'll generally track down titles on personal development.

While 85% of rich individuals read at least two personal growth books each month, just 11% read for diversion, contrasted with 79% of poor people. Furthermore, an incredible 94 percent of rich individuals read news distributions, contrasted with 11% of non-wealthy individuals.

Never totally resign:
The super-rich positively has sufficient money to never work one more day in their life, however, most of them continue to work, essentially

somewhat, frequently beyond 70. That doesn't mean they're timing long days at the workplace; without a doubt, they're most likely taking their reasonable portion of getaways and getting a charge out of adaptable timetables. However, numerous rich individuals never totally resign. This isn't because they can't stand to, but because they appreciate what they do.

Many are business visionaries on a basic level, and the craving to run and grow a business never leaves them. The dependability of working and the feeling of direction and satisfaction it gives them is a significant piece of their general bliss. Working provides them with a continuous sensation of accomplishment and an objective to keep them centered. Also that it keeps the money coming in.

Abstain from overspending:
While non-wealthy individuals dream about burning through money without stress, purchasing extravagant vehicles, huge houses, and costly garments, the rich comprehend that the more money you spend, the less you have. The wealthy wouldn't remain affluent long assuming they spent unnecessarily. Regardless of how much money you procure, you'll continuously be poor if you spend more than you make.

The rich perceive that the less you spend, the more money you need to develop your abundance. Remember that thriftiness is compared with your pay, a rich individual might spend substantially more than somebody who is viewed as working class. In any case, in relative terms, the rich will quite often be frugal, and they ensure they don't overspend.

Find an opportunity to reflect:
A large number of the independent rich invest energy in centered thinking consistently. Burning through 30 minutes (or more) in a tranquil space allows them to ponder their life and objectives, contemplate their well-being and connections, think about their vocation and monetary objectives,

and break down where they're at present and where they need to be. Decisive reasoning time is fundamental to remaining in front of the market and taking into account what changes might be coming to your direction.

This is additionally time to zero in on personal development and managing thoughts. Some might select journaling or writing to assist them with thinking of savvy fixes and thoughts. Simply ensure you're investing your energy in useful reasoning. Try not to squander your psychological energy on ruminations or negative idea circles that will make you rethink yourself. The rich don't.